Praise for Goodnight, Poet

"Rissa's paradisiac poetry reminded me of something I had forgotten: I love reading poems. The elegant way she intertwines words and emotions with such _____ _____ harkens me back to my y_____ _____ _____ ns and sonnets by little kno_____ _____ _____ ld have stopped to read Goo_____ _____ _____
~ Eric C. Lindstrom, best-selling author, The Skeptical Vegan and The Smart Parent's Guide to Raising Vegan Kids

"Rissa makes relationships sexy, intimacy and familiarity sensual, and luxuriates in the simple joy of a beautiful, elegantly-chosen word spoken from the right mouth. Between you and me, it was hot as f&*k."
~ Leslie Gray Streeter, journalist, Palm Beach Post and author, Black Widow

"With a grace and elegance that is characteristically hers, Miller's poems radiate warmth and tenderness. She invites you inside on a cold night; her words are the heat source that calms you, nourishes you, wraps you in blankets until you are comforted. Each poem is a deeply-felt meditation on this most exquisite human experience: love. A strong, eloquent new voice in poetry, she is one to watch."
~ Jennifer Green, author, Through the Wormhole

"Rissa has created a delightful collection of poems perfect for reading aloud. She has a way of painting images so expressively, they feel more than mere words. Some poems are sweet, others beautiful in their tranquility. One of my favorites is the emotionally powerful 1000. Home Cooking, much more than a poem, turns a simple discussion of food into something sensual and intoxicating. I've got to read some of these to my significant other."
~ A.L. Kaplan, poet and author, Star-Touched

"In *Goodnight, Poet*, Rissa evokes fully feminine, tactile sensitivities with rippling shades of warmth, intimacy, and eroticism. Like the delicate sheer morning fog, she enfolds her reader in the experience of love, physical and emotional. Using soft yet vibrant, sensorial language, Rissa coaxes meaning from whispered, fleeting moments as she opens our eyes to a multitude of rich, tiny wonders that too often pass unnoticed. This collection is inspirational and unparalleled; a perfect way for lovers to enhance their love and end their day."
~ Nancy J. Alexander, author, *Relentless, Seeing Double, Twisted Realms*

"Compelled by grace, Miller's poems set new heights to classic themes, and are enjoyable in company or solitude."
~ Virginia Petrucci, writer and poet, *Recipes and How-To's*

"*Goodnight, Poet*, three parts, feels like an evolution. Whether that evolution is of the poet or a thought, a memory, or an experience, there is a journey. Such a wonderful selection of sweet and sultry alongside reality, mixing with wonder, and how with the right person by your side, they can all co-exist. Opposites don't always have to disagree."
~ Joshua Zirger, screenwriter, *The Letter*

Goodnight, Poet

Poems to
Share
at Bedtime

Rissa Miller

ISBN 978-1-7326152-0-5
LCCN 2018908759

ANALYTICAL ARTIST
and Indigo

Analytical Artist & Indigo Productions
PO Box 8771
Elkridge, MD 21075-9998

Disclaimer
Thank you for buying an authorized version of this book.
Please do not reproduce, scan, copy, or distribute any part of
it without consent of the copyright holder. By complying with
copyright laws, you are allowing the poet, editor, and artists
who worked on this volume to get paid for their labors.
Artwork is work. Gracias!

Publication Notes
Hijacking Heaven, first published in *Pen-In-Hand* magazine, Jan. 2018
Bedtime Stories, first published in *Pen-In-Hand* magazine, July 2018

Cover Design & Interior Design Elements: Brent F. Kim
Editor: Peter G. Pollak
Cover Photography & Poet Headshot: Nathaniel Corn
Poet Hair and Make-up Styling: Jessica Lynn Baligush

Introduction

Ever since I was a teenager, I've loved reading poetry just before bed. The poems vary based on my mood, the time available, or simply what I discovered at the library.

Thirty-something years later, I still can't think of a sweeter farewell to the day than the singsong beauty of a poem.

When I married my husband Nathaniel, the tradition evolved into reading poems aloud. Sometimes he reads to me, sometimes I read to him. It's not always my original work. We share favorites both new and old.

I will always remember the night he first said it - I read him several favorites by William Carlos Williams. With a smile, Nathaniel leaned over, kissed me, and said "Goodnight, Poet." I loved him even more.

With this collection, I invite you into the fold. Cultivate a beautiful ritual of your own and embrace poetry at bedtime. Read to yourself, your partner, your animal companion. Start here, with these poems. Each was designed to reflect upon and share as the day unwinds.

All were written for people I love.

Contents

Part Three: Yes, My Love

to Nathaniel

Part One

For Your

Beloved

Shoulder

No one would describe my stance as strong.
From bone to bone, my shoulders measure fifteen slight inches.
Yet I can hold the weight of your heart.
Lean over, let your head drop
let your tears roll the narrow straits, scapula to spine.
Your grief soaks in, absorbed by a soul robust enough to steady.

My shoulders bear the crush of your sorrow,
tip your forehead to meet my collarbone,
breathe, yield to the strain. You are safe.
Arms only 20 inches - humerus, radius, ulna - fold you in,
fingers enfold in love and let loss languish.

Some might say they look too frail, bony.
These shoulders have been dislocated,
pinched into very tight places, even defeated.
But now they rise, they fortify against collapse.
Fall into me, I've got you.

I can, I will hold the weight of your heart.

Bedtime Stories

Most assuredly, there is a monster under your bed.
Starving, appetite yowling, yearning,
nails scrape into the hardwood floor
and strands of sticky drool drip down a leathery chin.
Such beasts roam the night,
eternal villains... fatigued by solitude.
They wish for the same as all, the same as you:
a friendly nod or warm glance with an exaggerated blink
that hints *I love you.*
Monsters such as the one under your bed
aren't crouching to attack, haunches spring-loaded
on bony ankles, unkempt wiry hair bristled.
In his time below your box spring
he sifted through the old family photos,
recognizes your Aunt Jo and all those cousins.
Nightly he examines a discarded menu from China Panda,
wonders if they really serve dragon, because he knows a few...
That random yellow sock you misplaced last spring
is his regular companion
as he flicks at dust bunnies with pointy claws.
Your monster waits for a tap against the side of the mattress
calling him to climb up and burrow into the blankets.
Couldn't you make room by the wall,
and let him arch against your back?
Your monster hungers for nearness and compassion,
a snuggle. Just a scratch behind his floppy ears.
He longs to know you see past fangs into
a soul that dreams of sharing the sofa on movie night,
a handful of popcorn to cherish,
and a goodnight kiss after bedtime stories.

Mid-Afternoon

Chickadee perches by the window
her feathery black mask a reverie of sunflower seeds
and dried cranberries.
Curled in a sofa nest under the worn throw,
my fingers cross the cup of chamomile,
flowery steam and sweet daisy dancing in the steep.

Catbird shoos the noisy grackle,
as if he senses me settling for a nap.
He knows I long to wrap in the blanket,
bundled for the repose of 20, 30, 40 winks.
Sipping tea, I silently promise blackberry
rewards for my capped-gray friend.

Beyond the still house, tranquil trees mellow.
Tea to the table, head to armrest,
I drift on gentle wings like swifts soaring
to a quiet lucid flight -
unruffled, mid-afternoon feathered in calm.

Yonder

When morning comes the breeze will hum at our window,
begging to play with your hair.
She will invite you to traverse the forest,
only stopping to reach into heaven and pluck
clouds like cherries from branches.
You wake and as your feet hit the ground
the soil sings,
eager to nestle your step
as twigs snap their beat - the music you love most.
Speeding through the trees,
you hear leaves summon... *Let me show you yonder.*
Because you know the river too well to fear the current
and each degree of dawn unveils the sepia majesty
of footprints on a muddy trail.
The waterfall bends her flow as you pass,
thirsting to rinse your sweat in her stormy prism.
Neighborhoods of squirrels, fox and all those
residents with feathers expect you at just past sunrise o'clock,
tails twitching, wings a loft.
You weave by, waving to the woodland clique,
lift into the slow incline that ascends a foggy meadow.
The steady beat of strides leads you
up staircases of roots and rocks and a hundred hovering pulses.
They create the rhythm of the run
and as you go by, a fern unfurls her fiddlehead fronds,
whispering
let me show you yonder.

How to Hug Me
for Shannon, Ben, Jeff & Brent

Dear friend, will you honor me once more with your arms?
I'm not longing for a hasty pat on the shoulder
not the embrace of a lover, nor the comfort of a parent.
Please know, I'm not ungrateful, each gesture is a gift.
This is an uncomplicated request, my dear:
Won't you press close, clutch me in your breath?
Not that awkward leaning out you save for strangers
nor the chest thump into bone for your bros.
Nourish me friend, as we enfold each other arm for arm.
Clasp me to you. Let your soul squeeze mine just a little,
fostering familiar comfort, an ally,
simply a heartfelt hug, as I offer back to you.

LOL

You make me burst out,
eye squinched,
gut clenched,
laughing from low
from the very source
that secures the soulspring.
You split my sides,
mouth wide open,
roar in mirth
whoop
snort
giggle,
I can't help myself.
The way you tell it,
the inside joke,
the outside grin,
banter,
brow cocked and light
light heart.
You communicate
wonder, amuse,
and I
cover my smile at first,
tee-hee,
then let loose
a howl to echo the essence
and even the breeze laughs
and knows
merriment,
delight
in you.

Minute Rice
for Leslie

The secret is
you don't have to follow directions.
On anything.
Always follow your heart, she said
as she moved effortlessly through her kitchen.

No, she paused,
Follow your instincts.
Your heart will sometimes be
wrong.
(Can you hand me that measuring cup?)
Skip the directions, though.

Except... with Minute Rice.
You have to follow the directions on Minute Rice.
If you don't measure it
just right
and cook it just so,
it's nasty.

Minute Rice is a sure thing.
The rest is an experiment.
Maybe your heart will always be wrong, you know?
Follow your mind.
Or just ask me,
because I love you.

Hijacking Heaven

Polaris belongs to me.
I have captured each star and store them
stuffed next to my thighs in blue jeans.
Polaris speaks to me the most. Chatterbox.
I reach into my pocket and sift through stardust.

People notice my fingers glow
with luminous splendor from the ancient sand,
old as time, old as God.
I cannot hide this secret.

I have stolen the stars.
Five galaxies away, someone is missing their star,
I'm sure of it.
Shadows stretch long in their world.
Nighttime rules and strange creatures emerge in the
everlast eventide.

Yeah, I hijacked Heaven -
and I count the seconds until the framework of our sky
might buckle.

Polaris told me many things, secrets whispered between angels,
of unfound life and new happiness.
I smile shyly at my yellow supergiant.
Polaris loves to talk, like the omniscient
old lady across everyone's street:
ready to share.

Tonight the moon eclipses red.
I need to send them home, the stars, and
wiggle back through the wormhole to stable orbit.
Polaris guides, the same for centuries, to the north and yonder
as I situate stars back in the sky.

The hard work is done, brilliance restored to dusk.
Now to conceal my cosmic clandestine felony.
The last evidence: scrub stardust from my fingernails.
But if you ever wonder, Polaris will tell.

It was me.
I stole the stars… and I kept one for you.

Witchcraft
to Willow

Miss is not in bed.
Invisible forces call her from the quilt and her silent toes
touch the ground.
Miss stands ready to read signs of the obscure.
Beloved moonlight reveals the path
towards the mythic world where cats spend their nights.

By day, you may not believe in magic.
The logic, the skeptic, you say that cats are simply cats.
Though what is that but logic?
Cats are indeed cats,
and Miss has charmed you so entirely, cast a spell so potent,
you fail to notice the coven that convenes in your garden.
They prance, raising the wind,
in fine calico, grey tiger stripes and thick black coats.

You've overlooked the feline to divine and now,
a witch has moved into the house.
She rests by you on the couch,
perches in your window by sunlight.
Miss tamed you with a purr
and makes her own demands - which you obey -
for feasts of tuna, cheese and catnip.

Miss placed the sacred sign upon your home,
blessing you from evil.
She is a wise woman, patrols your hallway,
stealthily passing the children's beds.
A positive force in the gloom,
her presence is your talisman.
The esoteric association between one world
and the next.

Tonight Miss is not in bed.
The dark is alive, witching hour has arrived.
Squinting into the shadows, you focus,
an attempt to share her vision.
However, you are not catlike.
Raised eyebrows and all, you will never perform her rites.
Only witches wake at this hour,
they anoint their charges with defense from the wicked.
Go back to sleep, human.
Miss prowls the night, she reads the signs.
Miss calls the wind to sing you into dreamland.

Chiaroscurist

(noun) artist who uses light and dark arrangements
in a pictorial work to create volume

We cannot deny the paradox of each other.
Your value greater than the sum of the shadows
as wealth is found in
the space between stark and start.
My incandescence announces the
interplay of dissimilar characters and
variations of slate emerge.
But in highlights and lowlights the
landscape of sameness is revealed:
You soften.
I glow.
We cannot exist in solitude.
The veil of dusk shelters
as ourselves blend into a burst of middle gray,
tones building dimension,
convergence of light and dark
complete the picture in lavish style.

Good Medicine

You fought the night
my brave, strong friend,
full force against the enemy.
Armed with vitamin C, broth, and
a cool cloth for your forehead
I soldier on for you.
This virus stands no chance.
If it keeps you up all night
it keeps me up all night.
Sneezy, achy, acutely sweaty
while too hot, too cold and too hot again
we march on, engaging both
fever and chills in a dogfight.
You wallow, say it's hard to breathe,
ears, nose and throat in dissension.
No one finds ease on the front line.
You act like it's the end,
but I'll drag you from the trenches
again
and again
until this cold gives up its ground.
Rest now. Let me handle the skirmish.
Burrow in your blankets and
know you have a reason to soldier on.

Shepherdess
to Gertrude, Patrick and Abby

Sleepless, some people imagine
a row of round woolly bodies
prancing over neat board fences.
They stride on small hooves, herding humans
towards slumber.
But ask yourself,
what's in it for the sheep?
Parade of neutral mundane,
their masks of black or honey brown
queued nose to tail.
Why wouldn't sheep prefer to press a soft muzzle
to your cheek, nod in contentment
as clouds linger across the moon?
Sheep know faces, they see you feelingly.
They wouldn't bypass a friend to patter
one by one till dawn
when they could choose to engulf you in
fuzzy nose kisses.
Not everyone can be a shepherdess.
You must allow a break in the procession,
protect them with each wiggly wag of their tails.
Sheep need rest, too.
How lucky at twilight when the sheep sniff your skin,
their nostrils a cozy tickle.
They huddle close in the lush fields of your heart,
curled shoulder to hock in the straw.
Weave your fingers in fleece,
ease into their gentle bleating as you drift
over worn fences through the open gate of dusk.

Part Two

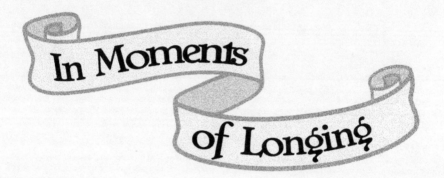

Piano Lesson

Slim long fingers strum lightly
in precise meter and pattern.
I watch blue veins, ivy under the sky,
as fingertips touch my wrist,
correct the arch and technique.
Here is a feline touch,
gently padding its way across
my hands, the click of nails
slightly audible on keys.
I hear you with learned passion:
Allegro, feverish,
all the way home
fading... fermata.

(In a dream, I am your piano.)

Nocturne

At three a.m. I wrap myself for warmth
in spinning lines and small, oblong enclosures
like sound on paper.
The delicate pattern
of bars cinch me to my instrument
and sadly strange bedfellows
become so familiar
they express the feeling behind God.
Now all the hot summer nights
I missed gather
behind long white curtains.
Wind loves to caress such vision
and I spread my hands across canyons
in fevered arpeggio -
each Romantic turns now in
his tomb, and groans softly to stretch for my passion.

I open so wide that the sound
might swallow every orgasm from
alone or company.
Each girl I know will sigh,
wondering why she must wait so long
for a kiss.
Liszt's long hair brushes my neck
as he bows prostrate down my body,
sits with me on the bench.
I see empty air.
We pass notes of solid flesh,
each to the other,
full of ideas we should never flesh out.
During the dry months, I visit here often.
When making love, I hear things speak music.

Ra

With only this necklace I approach for offering.
You watch my body. Eyes slit in darkness,
consume each quality of imperfection.

I rush forward in anxious homage,
anticipating reward granted to the pious,
but you hold like mist over the Nile.

This is no Egyptian temple I kneel before
yet air inhales, transports to a place
where sun stings the sand under knees of the faithful,
where such modest token may please.

Fingers tremble over the cord around my neck,
soft clink of metal to metal,
soft lilt of flesh to mouth in warm light luster.

To my deity I bring this simple string of beads,
an offering of common brass
across the hollow of my bare chest.

Here I worship.
Here I lean forward and fit my mouth to your navel,
such aurous skin as seen in ancient mosaic
such taste as salt a thousand seas.

I press a kiss behind your ear.
Ethereal touch, the necklace beckons,
yearning to adorn your heart.

Rocket

Tonight bows solitary before this orange moon.
I embrace cool sky glance,
wonder where you rest.
There is presently a lunar pull on the water.
Tides wash constellations in nocturnal lust,
store the romance of the Milky Way.
But I have nothing to do with the stars.
No moonbeam celestial light escapes these eyes.
In a galaxy of cosmic storybook lovers
my night is illuminated by you.
Light years from now you may come to me,
you may profess love,
you will not know,
might never know.
Ptolemy will never record this new
black hole in the heavens.
You see, I have nothing to do with the stars.
No half full quarter moon
shimmers across these waters.
This world is rare Earth, rooted deep,
with so much sky going up and up and out.
In the separation between,
Venus suffers permanent retrograde
and such clouds that consume.
Here is the space for we.
Domicile and hearth, structure made for launch.
And with this force, the lightning powers in from above.

Night Watch

You can't see the view from my window.
Miles from home, I wish we could share
the rows of pines around an
unfathomable cobalt bay.
Boats bob in the sendoff for sunshine,
the night watch passing to Mistress Moon.
She chaperones the shadows as they tiptoe
towards my balcony bannister,
envelop the vista, curtain falling
over a bloom of crimson, copper and coral light.

Miles from home, missing you and our
natural habitat of sofa, breezy window screen
and the dog's head resting on my lap
in the last breath of day.
If only my phone could offer you more:
evergreen perfume sheathed
in golden bright, ebb of the tide on a worn dock,
and my lips to your earlobe,
gently pressing a welcome home...

Because home is wherever you are.

1000

The bedroom ceiling hasn't changed.
Eyes wide, I watch the wooden beams.
Thank God they are strong,
they hold on, hold up.

The sheets are unoccupied to the left,
my fingers wanting the plane of your chest,
the gentle roll of your inhale.
No trace of your scent remains in the cotton
yet I breathe you even now,
wish I could whisper 1000 goodnights.
My lips part in unheard objection.
Not mine, you're not
for me.

I risk imagining the pass of your glance
down my back, bottom, legs,
wish for the weight of your body
pressed into mine.
Silent blue numbers on the nightstand
broadcast the time.

It's (too) late, when lovers gather
1000 ways: against the wall, the counter, the car.
Are you wrapped in another's legs tonight?
Someone else receives your dark strangling kisses,
scratch of your jawline,
three days unshaven across your cheek?

I long for the 1000 times
I will not hear your breath quicken in my ear.
Should I start a list?

Outline every moment you
made me fidget, blush,
laugh so hard my sides hurt?

Ardently I clasp my nails into my palms.
Pain obscures you
in the restless shift, though I hold -
so in love I shiver if someone says your name.
There were only 1000 moments I could have told you,
could have said yes and had you
between me and the stare of the empty ceiling.
But I am still here, still here.
Still...

Just Below Zero

You lie sleeping as I prepare to leave.
My fingertips trace your mouth, your throat,
the hollow behind your collar bones.
You do not feel my breath on your face.

Nothing is wrong.
No cloud cover,
no rain.
Through the window is a blue serenade
where each laugh we shared holds -
singing, wailing
with such poignant soul
I must cover my ears as I lean in for goodbye.

These eyes are ice blown far
and I await the permafrost gradually filling
my space on the sheet.
I touch your lashes with my lips.
You do not feel the frosty layer forming on your skin
as we drag down just below zero.

Waxing Puritanical

Vanilla tights
neatly pulled over thighs
smoothing upward, filling in
to a small navy skirt.
Seated in a second rate restaurant,
she shifts again - hair, eyes, blouse -
the blue across her lap
so suddenly small.

Over the table he greets
with nervous fingers handshake.
There is a shadow between
her legs he can't see
sweet cream not yet poured to the cup.
Her left hand covers
sugar frosted flesh,
subtly darkened rounds skimming to
almond alabaster.

Her fingers curl round the hem.
She nods shyly at his smile
and shifts again,
pulling on a fabric that
will not stretch
will not give her anymore.

Duende

(noun) mysterious power of art or dance
to deeply move and inspire

I am the lush red of apples in old masters paintings.
You long to bite the skin,
ripe like figs in autumn
and sweet to the secret core.
The pitcher of wine,
Cabernet chalice -
fragrant in thick layers of paint and pen.
The beauty right before you,
yet always out of reach,
leaving you drunk with enchanting improbabilities.

I am the painting
you look at and see your own meaning.
Your mirror, flattering,
I lift you, know you as well as destiny
knows you.
And goodness, how you sway,
you surrender your power.
I am the air, the oil and pigment,
the medium of your hunger,
fruit that fills you up
as if you had no idea there was so much space
to love…

Muse

When the lock clicks on the office door,
I shed these familiar brown frame glasses
and loosen the ties on my hair.
Black lace garters rested all day under
my plain gray suit and I trade sensible flats for
crimson velvet crush.
Haven't you guessed about me?
I like to look at girls,
watch their practiced walk.
They watch the other girls,
They struggle with their shoes.
Tight shirts, tight skirts
a seamless flow of hands
on hips, the curve of thigh to bottom.
Tonight to find a girl find a boy find a friend.
Invite me down the small of your back?
Keep opening till you unravel,
vanished in the tangle of reverence and lush,
very yes, but not lost in you, Muse.
Lipstick press and press together
It took four shades of pink to pout like this -

And boys just sit... and look at girls.

Part Three

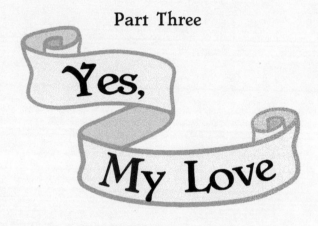

Yes, My Love

Begin

In the first moment, you gasp
as if my flicker filled your lungs, and sadness
must be coughed out like sickness.

Raise your face just a bit and
uplift dust filters in my shimmer.
Slouched from your eyes
to your waist, watching the ground pass
for years, until you lift your chin,
startled and blinking to see me, the sky,
waiting for you all along.

Extracted from the shade of the shadows,
you shiver, heave, ablaze in resplendent glow,
illuminated from the depth of my adoration.
Inhale again, Beautiful, notice your becoming.

Recognize at once the one who perceives you,
knows just how to ignite you.

That last inch up,
I push my hair behind my ear
to greet your gaze.
We cross the intersection
we both knew would light upon us all along.

Birthright

Someone claimed you, the psychic said
as her fingers hovered over my lap.
There is an S on your inner thigh…
Yes ~ (How did she know?!)

Since birth, a small mark, simple stroke of S
secret inscription between my legs.
A mark no doubt placed as a reminder,
of a pledge made between souls.

Your name, however, has no S.
Not one, not anywhere.
I tell her she is mistaken,
I recognize no prophecy nor lost hero.

The sage insists His name starts with S.
Yet no Sam Shane or Samir appeared to love me.
Could it be my cafe au lait imprint
was the breath of an angel whispering his pact?

I picture the conspiratorial birthright,
the signature on my left leg,
but Scott Sean Stephan dawdled, delayed.
You arrived first, took what you desired.

First or last name, I ask, considering an
undisclosed Mr. Smith Sanchez Sullivan
in sub rosa declaration bestowed and now broken -
the S unseen, deep between my thighs.

You were promised and a mark was made.
He searches still, his soul cannot dismiss so easily.

She shakes her head, brow pinched.
(But how did she know about that birthmark?)

S stands for stolen swiped snatched.
The space now occupied by you, my love,
because when Stan Sebastian Spencer shows up
I am already yours.

Stargazing

You're considering a tattoo on your shoulder
in what I like to think of as the Orion system,
located between here and here on your skin.

My universe, your skin, all alive, sweet,
the multiverse of you-ness.
A rose, you say, or perhaps a chain of ivy?

An alien invader of my eternal constellations,
the freckles that trail your arms and neck.
Recognizable patterns and forms create legends across you.

Often my mouth leads me to the system of Andromeda.
Will the sword of Perseus cut me down, I wonder
as I glide along your spine, breathtaking distinctive flecks
already marking you, lovelier that the goddess herself.

Hers, a story of a beauty brought down by boasts.
The night sky holds 88 such tales.
Your body, though, so many more, each ever new to explore.

Centaur points his arrow, and you ask
What about a heart or a word, something with meaning?
I try to imagine it etched in ink on the cosmos.

At the edge of your neck, my lips connect stars, you to me.
Stargazing into the darkness, I encounter ruling planet Venus
as you settle on infinity.

Moonrise

The magnolia tree offers a personal greeting
as we meander the garden path.

Each bloom kissed by rain,
a languorous pass of petals and leaves -
vines growing to the ground.

Your hands are full of flowers and you tell me,
We are not immune to beauty.

Deep beneath, seeds nudge into soil
as we linger under entwined branches and heaven.

Eager as the crocus, unfolding like the iris,
I am collected in your bouquet.

(whisper)

Some words should be whispered,
like when you ask your friend
for a Twizzler in the movie theater
(Can I have one of those?)
or when your co-worker's nose hair
sticks out going to a meeting.
(Psst.. you might want to handle that.)
Some say it's rude to whisper,
that if you can't say it loud, why speak at all?
As if a secret must be tinged with insinuation,
hints of suspicion hidden in plain breath.

Not all whispers are boycotts, however.
Lovers murmur across the shared pillow,
each sigh precious, a disclosure inviting
the other to a private feast.
These moments are confidences
amplified by the lull.
Sometimes, you whisper to me
and we are a celebration of hush,
roving towards a spree of volume unknown.
(Will you kiss me again?)

Home

Fuzzy slippers nuzzle toe to toe beside the bed.
They're like us, snug as a hound by the hearth
familiar as the threadbare robe after a bath.

Huddled into your lanky frame,
still wrapped in sheets and legs and blankets
after years of goodnights.

We share the ease of intimately knowing,
embody the comfort of habit.

Each night you lift the duvet and hold me
like a vase welcoming a rose,
repeating the melt of love that last.

the Dance

The simple beauty of being
yours
us
together
is enough to make me rise from the bench.
Because I like this song,
I ask you to dance.
Now
here
next to the sofa, in old clothes and flip-flops.
The singer knows a thing or two
about love.
She says so,
enraptured lyrics
a caress of chords
and harmony.
You wrap me in your arms
face bowed to my hair.
Sometimes
you step on my feet.
But I do the same,
because it's like that.
You can't always know the
right place to
stand.
Which is fine by me.
The dance itself
is the destination.
Let's glide and twirl
and so long as we both shall live,
please promise we can
always
slow dance
in the living room.

the Red Fan

For 45 cents, I found a fan in New Orleans,
second hand relief for the summer swelter.
As the hot flutters from my face,
I imagine who owned this beauty last.

Were the half dozen daisies admired by a child?
Perhaps she played dress up with Momma's high heels
and a skirt from the back of the closet, fanning herself
in a display of sophistication.

The fan ruffles my hair, increasing cool on my skin
gentle air winding to you across the sheets.
The red tassel grazes your belly
as I picture the fingers of another woman,

she clutches the fan by its chipped gold edge,
refreshing herself, yet coquetteish before her suitor.
Rigorous back and forth of her arm makes her
breasts sway slightly...
Can this small folding fan displace so much spark?

I wonder as I study the painted red paper stretched over slats,
the simple cross section of a circle
combined with motion. Such a small gesture, yet
release from the oppression of a New Orleans afternoon.

My legs rest around you like the guardstands of the fan,
swooped on the pivot. I see lovers for centuries, hand fans
to taper the heat, thousands of breezes lighten the room,
yet cannot not blow away our warmth.

Dangle

Spirals and beads corkscrew
long earrings.
At a street festival, I stop -
Can't you see these on me?
Silver coils glint in the afternoon glare.
They dangle to my shoulders,
connected circles
jump ring to fine chain,
inches long, swinging freely with
jingle-clink-chitter.
I am just right with metal sweeping my throat,
long hair tossed side to front.
Can't you see me in these earrings, I ask,
and nothing else?

Thieves in the Morning

You pull me from computer and coffee
as I tell you good morning, it's time
for work.
But you have another job in mind.
Time stolen from sunlight
in a highly suspect raid.

Start here, my neck, my mouth
I clothe you in breathlessness as I wonder…
perhaps you are wanted for crimes against midnight?
Looting the dark of her mystery
we are thieves in the morning,
glistening with sweat, naked in sunshine.

One mile east, the good people
of our city line the beltway, offices attendant.
Should I call the boss, say I forgot some appointment?
Do I show up, messy hair and pink cheeks
still flush from the smash and grab?

We fall backwards to seduce the early bright.
Brilliant sunrise surges the window.
This, our morning rush hour.
(Perhaps we take two?)

Home Cooking

When I offer you the plate,
my love tastes like peaches
soft and sweet and wet,
the lightest kiss of summer.
Plucked ripe from the tree.
Give me your mouth.
Sink in to the flesh.
Just like that I am inside you.
Eating, the only intimate act
that truly makes you who you are.

As I hand you the bowl,
know my love burns like slow curry
stirred with cayenne, star anise and cardamom.
Intoxicating heady aroma will
fascinate and I ask, can you savor
my skin the same? What if you
brush your tongue across my wrist -
salt seasons the dish.

Walk with me to the kitchen,
you can help with dinner.
Wrap your fingers round
to squeeze the juice,
each drop precious into the dough.
All bread must rise, given time,
a little moisture and
something to consume.
The ideal texture is airy but firm,
you know...

When you open to take that bite,
know my love simmers at your melting point.
I will sautease you to the crush.

Chew slowly, taste each syllable.
Prized as saffron,
strong as cast iron.
Uncommon offering in a very well-melded marinade.

Please walk with me to the kitchen
where you can read the love letter
I wrote in cinnamon bark,
toasted cumin,
and Meyer citrus peel.
It will steam you tender crisp,
leave you baked and bound.
If you like, you can taste my love for yourself.

Just eat my words.

Nectar

Other lips have touched mine,
but none have kissed me since you left
my mouth wet
with sweet mango gloss.
The ambrosia delight,
key lime twist that tastes like you.
Should I beg, plead for the dream of
papaya, starfruit and kiwi,
juicy sweet flesh and pulp,
so hot I can hear the fruit sweat?
Slide your mouth across mine,
kiss me again, tropical crush -
I can't cut loose, can't forget the
luscious nectar of your balmy lips.

Slow You Go

Over and over
I comprehend
thankful,
that love is not candied
or clean,
neither plain nor precise,

but extraordinary
unthinkable,
and bitter,
scattered and full,
with turbulence
ecstasy
ruckus
and smitten bites like
jewels of chocolate and raspberry.

Everyday, slow you go,
turning the world of ours
over in your hands
again and again,
real life with
dirty dishes, dirty minds, dirty chai
and slow we go
as we allow this love
to root and wind,
ours.

Goodnight, Poet

Profoundly unaware of immense waves surrounding the boat,
I am another Pisces wandering deep in the aquamarine. As
always, you sense my departure, my delve into the world of
words. A plot, a poem, some new tale to tell with a flawed hero
or crafty queen.

You spy me loose in the crushing clear, awash in luxurious
depth, drifting to open sea. Mermaids swim by my side,
submerged fantasy with rush and roll. Sirens beckon me
forward. My breath to bubbles, I plunge hard seeking the
next clue to unlock the treasure. Rippling through the limitless
majesty of wavy, wondrous blue, I venture farther into
briny mist.

Part of me knows it's critical to turn back, remember the way
home. As always, you initiate the rescue operation. Pull me
into the net. The catch contains my dreams of poetry, awe, and
fright. You, beside me, the anchor…

Rolling over in bed, you gesture to the notepad in my hand,
stroke my hair, and kiss my forehead. As always, you say,
Goodnight, Poet.

Goodnight, Reader
xoxo Rissa

Book Club Questions and Topics

From Part One

1) Shoulder: Does trust already exist between the two people in this poem? Why or why not?

2) Bedtime Stories: What is the monster under the bed? Is he a literal monster or could there be parallel meanings?

3) Yonder: How does the natural world make the runner come alive? *Discussion Idea* ~ For those who love nature walks, camping or trail running, how does the forest feel like home?

4) How to Hug Me: *Discussion Idea* ~ How many kinds of hugs can you think of? What defines a comforting, comfortable hug for you?

5) Hijacking Heaven: Polaris is the North Star, used for centuries as guide for sailing. Of all the stars, why would Polaris be the one to talk the most? What might Polaris know? What do the stars represent in the poem?

6) Minute Rice: *Discussion Idea* ~ Is anything in life a simple guarantee of success, like Minute Rice?

7) Witchcraft: *Discussion Idea* ~ At many points in history, cats were associated with witchcraft. How do cats, in their usual behaviors, reinforce this ancient stereotype? Do you think the cat in the poem possesses any supernatural power?

8) Chiaroscurist: Written about a black and white photograph, this poem reaches past the original picture that inspired it. How does the idea of middle gray and sameness speak to creating volume in one's life?

9) Shepherdess: Why would sheep leave a flock and line up one by one to be counted? Do you think sheep, like dogs or cats, might enjoy cuddling?

From Part Two

10) Piano Lesson: What is the subject of adoration? The pianist? The music itself?

11) Nocturne: *Discussion Idea* ~ This poem was written about a performance of Liszt's *Campanella*. How does music truly sit with you and physically manifest, as suggested in the poem?

12) Ra: Is the worshipper aware of their lover's humanity? How and why do they relate their lover to Ra, the Egyptian Sun God?

13) Rocket: Who is the traveler? Does it matter if they ever come home?

14) 1000: Has the relationship in 1000 ended - or did it never start? Does longing manifest as love or lust in this piece?

15) Just Below Zero: Is this poem about a person alive or dead?

16) Waxing Puritanical: What kind of meeting might these two people be engaged in? What else is happening between them?

17) Duede: *Discussion Idea* ~ Can you think of artwork that moved you, inspired you, or changed your perception? What made it powerful? How are poems like paintings?

From Part Three

18) Begin: What started in this poem? Is this a true first meeting, or do these people already know each other?

19) Birthright: *Discussion Idea* ~ Have you ever been to a psychic or had a tarot reading? What did you think?

20) Moonrise: What does "we are not immune to beauty" mean to you? How does this play out in the poem and/or in life?

21) (whisper): *Discussion Idea* ~ Are there right and wrong times to whisper?

22) the Dance: If the dance itself is the destination, does it follow that where it's done or where the dancers step doesn't matter? How does this reflect life?

23) Home Cooking: *Discussion Idea* ~ Do you agree that eating is the only intimate act that makes you who you are? How can eating or cooking be intimate?

24) Nectar: *Discussion Idea* ~ What is the effect of the smell and/or taste of a kiss?

25) Goodnight, Poet: How does the poet experience a flow state in this piece? What is the value of remaining grounded in such a creative mind space?

Do you organize a Book Club?

Rissa would be glad to join the discussion via Skype if your group reads *Goodnight, Poet* as a featured selection. Reach out to her at www.rissawrites.com for availability.

Acknowledgements

Thanks to my husband, Nathaniel. If you hadn't loved me - and believed in me - this collection would never have happened.

Thanks to my friends at critique group: Robin, Susan, Peter and Mark. Your insights keep me honest and make me so much better. Additional feedback came from Paloma and from the past, thanks to Rick.

Very big thanks to my hugely talented designer, Brent, and kind editor, Peter. Both of you made a lot of time for this project and you worked hard to make me look good. Gracias! Thanks to Brooke, ace copy editor and so much more. Cindy gets a big shout out ~ lots of support all the way through.

Thanks to Jeff, who allowed me to read after his yoga classes, and the members of the Mud Not Blood vegan running team. You listened to these poems for months and helped me hear them clearly. Jess and Nancy deserve special mention, as well as the good people at One World Cafe.

Thanks to the folks at Maryland Writers Association, Root Studio, David's Vegan Buffet & Open Mic, Spiral Staircase Poetry, Vegan Book Club, and Wilde Readings. All of you politely applauded, even when my hands were trembling on the pages as I got used to reading publicly again.

So many friends have read poems and offered me advice, thoughts, encouragement - you know who you are and you know that I love and appreciate you.

About the Poet

Rissa loves hot green tea in antique cups, lingering walks through the produce department, and paying compliments to strangers. Everyday life is her constant inspiration for writing poems, plays, fiction, essays, and recipes. Rissa is a vegan of 23 years and is currently the senior editor at *Vegetarian Journal* magazine. She studied writing at New York University and photojournalism at Western Kentucky University. With her husband Nathaniel and their Spanish greyhound companion, Valerio, Rissa makes her home in Maryland.

Visit her at www.rissawrites.com

Love it? Like it? Hate it?

Thank you for reading this poetry collection! Many hours were poured onto these pages for your enjoyment. It's an honor you made the time to read it.

If you will, leave a review for Rissa on Amazon or Goodreads. Honest feedback is a critical part of growth for all creatives.

If you liked - or loved - *Goodnight, Poet*, tell a friend, give a copy as a gift, share it on social media, or suggest it to your Book Club. These may sound like small gestures, but the tiniest act of kindness from readers can make or break the career of an author.

Every online review and word of mouth recommendation makes a difference! Thanks!

THE SWEEP

Free online now at www.rissawrites.com

Step into the world four years after an engineered virus crushes modern society. In this post-apocalyptic thriller series, self-taught healer Mercy struggles through the treachery of uncivilized wilderness as she realizes there are pieces of the past she cannot run from, despite losing much of her memory in The Sweep. Meanwhile, unsettling forces discover Mercy holds the key to restoring the threads of humanity that give people memories. Will she survive, or will the cure be lost forever?

Cupcakes and Kisses

Coming Summer 2019
Rissa's first full-length novel!

Andi Grace has a great guy, who just proposed, and she co-owns a successful cupcakery with her two best friends. She thinks she has life figured out. When her high school crush appears, almost a decade after a car accident took him from prom and graduation, Andi isn't prepared to fall in love with someone deeply connected to her past. In this fun, funny, and real romantic comedy, revel in the beauty of imperfection – and loads of delectable treats!

THE DEVIL'S BOUDOIR

Coming Halloween 2019

Enter a seduction that leads you from a dusky cemetery, to the vampire's lair, through a witch's sacred circle and all the way to the bedchamber of the devil himself. This narrative poem collection will bring you to face-to-face with nightmares and ultimately dares you to confront a captivating temptress in a battle for your soul.

CPSIA information can be obtained
at www.ICGtesting.com
Printed in the USA
FSHW01n1536080918